Introduction - Why keep a Gratitude Journal?

This world we live in is filled with much negativity and it is easy to get bogged down and consumed with it. Personally, I have experienced physical and emotional challenges that have been painful and scaring. One of the most significant tools I have discovered in my search for healing, is keeping a Gratitude Journal. This daily commitment is a time to reflect on the amazing and positive things happening in life. It has provided me great strength that continues to grow day by day.

Below are the four categories in my journal:
1.) Inspiration 2.) Self-Affirmation
3.) Gratitude 4.) Success.

My prayer is that others will benefit from keeping their own gratitude journal. That they, too, will experience how life changing it can be.

-Amy Greiner

What do I write in my journal?

This is your journal. There are no do's and dont's on what to write. Below are some tips for each category. You will find some examples on the following four pages. Feel free to use them to help you get started.

Inspiration quotes: This can be a Bible verse or inspirational quote that is meaningful to you.

Self-Affirmation: State something positive about yourself.

Gratitude: Jot down something you are grateful for. It can be anything, there are no rules.

Success: Successes of **any** kind. Reflect on accomplishments made and acknowledge them!

Inspiration quotes

- All things work together for good...**Romans 8:28**
- The number one skill in life is not giving up. **Bryant McGill**
- Come to me, all who are weary and burdened and I will give you rest...**Matthew 11:28**
- There is nothing in nature that blooms all year long, so don't expect yourself to do so either. **Author Unknown**
- Integrity gives you real freedom because you have nothing to fear since you have nothing to hide. **Zig Ziglar**
- Cast all your anxiety on Him because He cares for you.
1 Peter 5:7
- When you focus on the good, the good gets better.
Abraham Hicks
- I can do all things through Christ who gives me strength. **Philippians 4:13**
- We don't remember days, we remember moments.
Cssare Pavese

Self-Affirmations

- I know exactly who I am. I am strong, brave, resilient, and unbreakable. I am a survivor.
- I do not accept negativity. I choose to see the positive things in life.
- My life is mine. I am in control of my choices. I refuse to allow outside influences cause me to self-doubt.
- I will continue to filter thoughts and fears...reminding myself that fears are false.
- I can take anything that comes my way. I'm not afraid because God is for me, not against me.
- Jesus is my first love. I do not need the approval of others.
- I am special and uniquely designed by God.
- I have confidence in myself and in the Lord.
- The things that other people do and say, do not define me or have an affect on my happiness.
  I choose to see the positive side of things - especially in myself. Its ok to think kindly of myself.
- Disappointments and setbacks may happen, but
  I will not allow my life to fall apart because of them. I have great strength and will live a happy, fulfilling life.

Gratitude

- Enjoyed spending time with my family at church..
- For tools I have learned to help me cope in difficult times.
- So grateful for the time with my children yesterday. It was a great Mother's Day!
- The Lord and how He guides me.
- Going to my son's last HS concert. Time has flown!.
- Special mother-daughter time with my daughter.
- God giving me the ability to take charge of my own health and strengthening me.
- Seeing my son graduate, I am so happy for him!
- Awesome and encouraging sermon yesterday. We have to be whole before we can have good, intimate relationships with other people.
- So thrilled for my daughter and her new job, she seems to really enjoy it!
- The love and care of my amazing family.
- The beautiful family ranch - my favorite place in the world!
- Music!
- A nice hot bubble bath.
- Quiet mornings drinking coffee and having my devotions.

Successes

- Bills paid, filing done, dressed, bedroom swept, and ready early.
- Had a tough day, but was able to stay strong.
- Making progress on my "to do" list
- Even after a tearful moment, I was able to lift my chin up and attend a meeting.
- Bathroom cleaned, dinner cooked, dogs to the vet, devotions done!
- Took care of many miscellaneous tasks that I have been pushing off to the side.
- Everyday - no matter the challenges or struggles, I am victorious, Christ lives and moves and breathes in me. He's the reason I keep getting up everyday.
- Able to shift focus yesterday and enjoy my son's moment.
- I am an overcomer and able to take on any challenge laid out before me.
- Able to redirect negative thoughts and remind myself of who I am and how strong I am.

Date

Inspiration

Self-Affirmation

Gratitude

Success

Date

Inspiration

Self-Affirmation

Gratitude

Success

Date

Inspiration

Self-Affirmation

Gratitude

Success

Date

Inspiration

Self-Affirmation

Gratitude

Success

Date

Inspiration

Self-Affirmation

Gratitude

Success

Date

Inspiration

Self-Affirmation

Gratitude

Success

Date

Inspiration

Self-Affirmation

Gratitude

Success

Date

Inspiration

Self-Affirmation

Gratitude

Success

Date

Inspiration

Self-Affirmation

Gratitude

Success

Date

Inspiration

Self-Affirmation

Gratitude

Success

Date

Inspiration

Self-Affirmation

Gratitude

Success

Date

Inspiration

Self-Affirmation

Gratitude

Success

Date

Inspiration

Self-Affirmation

Gratitude

Success

Date

Inspiration

Self-Affirmation

Gratitude

Success

Date

Inspiration

Self-Affirmation

Gratitude

Success

Date

Inspiration

Self-Affirmation

Gratitude

Success

Date

Inspiration

Self-Affirmation

Gratitude

Success

Date

Inspiration

Self-Affirmation

Gratitude

Success

Date

Inspiration

Self-Affirmation

Gratitude

Success

Date

Inspiration

Self-Affirmation

Gratitude

Success

Date

Inspiration

Self-Affirmation

Gratitude

Success

Date

Inspiration

Self-Affirmation

Gratitude

Success

Date

Inspiration

Self-Affirmation

Gratitude

Success

Date

Inspiration

Self-Affirmation

Gratitude

Success

Date

Inspiration

Self-Affirmation

Gratitude

Success

Date

Inspiration

Self-Affirmation

Gratitude

Success

Date

Inspiration

Self-Affirmation

Gratitude

Success

Date

Inspiration

Self-Affirmation

Gratitude

Success

Date

Inspiration

Self-Affirmation

Gratitude

Success

Date

Inspiration

Self-Affirmation

Gratitude

Success

Date

Inspiration

Self-Affirmation

Gratitude

Success

Date

Inspiration

Self-Affirmation

Gratitude

Success

Date

Inspiration

Self-Affirmation

Gratitude

Success

Date

Inspiration

Self-Affirmation

Gratitude

Success

Date

Inspiration

Self-Affirmation

Gratitude

Success

Date

Inspiration

Self-Affirmation

Gratitude

Success

Date

Inspiration

Self-Affirmation

Gratitude

Success

Date

Inspiration

Self-Affirmation

Gratitude

Success

Date

Inspiration

Self-Affirmation

Gratitude

Success

Date

Inspiration

Self-Affirmation

Gratitude

Success

Date

Inspiration

Self-Affirmation

Gratitude

Success

Date

Inspiration

Self-Affirmation

Gratitude

Success

Date

Inspiration

Self-Affirmation

Gratitude

Success

Date

Inspiration

Self-Affirmation

Gratitude

Success

Date

Inspiration

Self-Affirmation

Gratitude

Success

Date

Inspiration

Self-Affirmation

Gratitude

Success

Date

Inspiration

Self-Affirmation

Gratitude

Success

Date

Inspiration

Self-Affirmation

Gratitude

Success

Date

Inspiration

Self-Affirmation

Gratitude

Success

Date

Inspiration

Self-Affirmation

Gratitude

Success

Date

Inspiration

Self-Affirmation

Gratitude

Success

Date

Inspiration

Self-Affirmation

Gratitude

Success

Date

Inspiration

Self-Affirmation

Gratitude

Success

Date

Inspiration

Self-Affirmation

Gratitude

Success

Date

Inspiration

Self-Affirmation

Gratitude

Success

Date

Inspiration

Self-Affirmation

Gratitude

Success

Date

Inspiration

Self-Affirmation

Gratitude

Success

Date

Inspiration

Self-Affirmation

Gratitude

Success

Date

Inspiration

Self-Affirmation

Gratitude

Success

Date

Inspiration

Self-Affirmation

Gratitude

Success

Date

Inspiration

Self-Affirmation

Gratitude

Success

Date

Inspiration

Self-Affirmation

Gratitude

Success

Date

Inspiration

Self-Affirmation

Gratitude

Success

Date

Inspiration

Self-Affirmation

Gratitude

Success

Date

Inspiration

Self-Affirmation

Gratitude

Success

Date

Inspiration

Self-Affirmation

Gratitude

Success

Date

Inspiration

Self-Affirmation

Gratitude

Success

Date

Inspiration

Self-Affirmation

Gratitude

Success

Date

Inspiration

Self-Affirmation

Gratitude

Success

Date

Inspiration

Self-Affirmation

Gratitude

Success

Date

Inspiration

Self-Affirmation

Gratitude

Success

Date

Inspiration

Self-Affirmation

Gratitude

Success

Date

Inspiration

Self-Affirmation

Gratitude

Success

Date

Inspiration

Self-Affirmation

Gratitude

Success

Date

Inspiration

Self-Affirmation

Gratitude

Success

Date

Inspiration

Self-Affirmation

Gratitude

Success

Date

Inspiration

Self-Affirmation

Gratitude

Success

Date

Inspiration

Self-Affirmation

Gratitude

Success

Date

Inspiration

Self-Affirmation

Gratitude

Success

Date

Inspiration

Self-Affirmation

Gratitude

Success

Date

Inspiration

Self-Affirmation

Gratitude

Success

Date

Inspiration

Self-Affirmation

Gratitude

Success

Date

Inspiration

Self-Affirmation

Gratitude

Success

Date

Inspiration

Self-Affirmation

Gratitude

Success

Date

Inspiration

Self-Affirmation

Gratitude

Success

Date

Inspiration

Self-Affirmation

Gratitude

Success

Date

Inspiration

Self-Affirmation

Gratitude

Success

Date

Inspiration

Self-Affirmation

Gratitude

Success

Date

Inspiration

Self-Affirmation

Gratitude

Success

Date

Inspiration

Self-Affirmation

Gratitude

Success

Date

Inspiration

Self-Affirmation

Gratitude

Success

Date

Inspiration

Self-Affirmation

Gratitude

Success

Date

Inspiration

Self-Affirmation

Gratitude

Success

Date

Inspiration

Self-Affirmation

Gratitude

Success